Go Programming Language
Easy Guide Book

Table of Contents

Introduction

Go programming language is very important for creation of apps. The language is known for its ease of use. It is quick for one, even those new to programming, to grasp the concepts of the Go programming language and begin to create their own apps. Recently, Go version 1.6 was released and is now available on the market. This version of Go has brought in new techniques, and there is a need for you to learn how to use these techniques. This book guides you on how to use these techniques.

Chapter 1- Overview

Go is a programming language written for the purpose of supporting systems programming. The language was first released in the year 2007 at Google by Ken Thompson, Robert Griesemer, and Rob Pike. The language is statically and strongly typed, and supports concurrent programming, and inbuilt garbage collection. To construct programs in Go, we use packages, and this makes it easy for us to manage dependencies.

The implementation of the Go programming language makes use of the traditional compile and link model for the purpose of generation of executable models. The compilation of this language takes a very short time to run. The language has been made much simpler by the exclusion of features such as inheritance, but the available features have been made very easy for anyone to implement. In this book, we will explore the features of the Go programming language, release 1.6.

Chapter 2- Fetching URLs Concurrently

Go programming language supports a very interesting feature named *"concurrent programming."* Consider the example given below:

```
// Fetchall will fetch the URLs in parallel and then report their sizes and //times.
 package main
 import (
   "fmt"
   "io"
   "io/ioutil"
   "os"
   "time"
 )
 func main() {
   start := time.Now()
   ch := make(chan string)
   for _, url := range os.Args[1:] {
     go fetch(url, chn) // starting the goroutine
   }
   for range os.Args[1:] {
     fmt.Println(<-chn) // receiving from the channel chn
   }
   fmt.Printf("%.2fs                    elapsed\n", time.Since(start).Seconds())
 }
 func fetch(url string, chan chan<- string) {
   start := time.Now()
   resp, err := http.Get(url)
   if err != nil {
     chn <- fmt.Sprint(err) // sending to the channel chn
     return
   }
   nbytes, err := io.Copy(ioutil.Discard, resp.Body)
   resp.Body.Close() // avoid leaking of resources
   if err != nil {
```

```
    chn <- fmt.Sprintf("while reading %s: %v", url,
err)
    return
}
secs := time.Since(start).Seconds()
chn <- fmt.Sprintf("%.2fs  %7d  %s", secs, nbytes,
url)
}
```
The property *"fetchall"* will fetch the URLs, not one, but many, and this will be done concurrently. Because of this, much time will be saved. The *"goroutine"* is a function which is to be executed concurrently. The *"channel"* is just a communication mechanism which will allow one goroutine to pass the values of a specific type to another goroutine. The function *"main"* will run in the goroutine, and the statement *"go"* will create additional routines. The *"main"* function will use *"make"* so as to create a channel of strings.

Chapter 3- HTTP/2 and Go

Go 1.6 now supports the use of HTTP/2. This is an indication that we will be in a position to create servers in HTTP/2 without having to call the function *"ConfigureServer()."* HTTP/2 is a new version of the HTTP protocol, and it has brought about extra functionalities such as header compression and connection multiplexing. There are numerous libraries in Go which can be used for the purpose of creation of HTTP/2 servers.

Creating an HTTP/2 Server

It is easy for us to use the library http2 so as to create a server. This library will be integrated with the http package in our standard library. We will have to call the function *"http2.ConfigureServer()"* which will open a normal http server for us. We will then configure this server to use a http2 server. If you need to use the browser to access your server, you will have to configure an encryption of type TLS, and if you fail to do that, it will get back to using HTTP1.x. Although you don't need the encryption much, no browser supports the use of HTTP/2 in unencrypted form. This is shown in the code given below:

```
package main
import (
  "log"
  "net/http"
  "os"

  "golang.org/x/net/http2"
)
func main() {
  cwd, error := os.Getwd()
  if error != nil {
    log.Fatal(error)
  }
  srv := &http.Server{
    Addr:   ":8000", // Normally ":443"
```

```go
        Handler: http.FileServer(http.Dir(cwd)),
    }
    http2.ConfigureServer(srv, &http2.Server{})
    log.Fatal(srv.ListenAndServeTLS("server.crt",
"server.key"))
}
```

Creating an HTTP/2 Client

This is simply done by calling the object "http2.Transport."
This is then passed from the http package to the normal client.
The code given below best demonstrates this:

```go
package main
import (
  "fmt"
  "io/ioutil"
  "log"
  "net/http"
  "golang.org/x/net/http2"
)
func main() {
  client := http.Client{
    // InsecureTLSDial is just temporary and it may
later be
    // replaced by a different API.
    Transport:    &http2.Transport{InsecureTLSDial:
true},
  }
  resp, error := client.Get("https://localhost:8000/")
  if error != nil {
    log.Fatal(error)
  }
  body, error := ioutil.ReadAll(resp.Body)
  if error != nil {
    log.Fatal(error)
  }
  fmt.Println(string(body))
}
```

Constants

Consider the code given below:

```
const (
    // ClientPreface is our string which must be sent by the new
    // connections from our clients.
    ClientPreface = "PRI * HTTP/2.0\r\n\r\nSM\r\n\r\n"
    // NextProtoTLS is our NPN/ALPN protocol negotiated during the
    // HTTP/2's TLS setup.
    NextProtoTLS = "h2"
)
```

```
const TrailerPrefix = "Trailer:"
```

Once we use TrailerFix as shown in the above case, it indicates that the map entry is simply for the response trailers, but not for the response headers. The prefix will be stripped once the the call ServeHTTP has been finished and all the values have been sent into the trailers.

This kind of mechanism is only for trailers which are not known before the headers are implemented. If we are aware of the trailers before the implementation of the headers, it is good for us to stick to the normal style of trailers in Go programming language.

Variables

These can be declared as shown below:

var DebugGoroutines = os.Getenv("DEBUG_HTTP2_GOROUTINES") == "1"

var ErrFrameTooLarge = errors.New("http2: frame is too large")

The "ErrFrameTooLarge" will be returned from the "Framer.ReadFrame" once the peer has sent a frame which is larger than the "SetMaxReadFrameSize." This is shown in the code given below:

var ErrNoCachedConn = errors.New("http2: no found cached connection")
var (
  VerboseLogs bool
)

With the methof *"ConfigureServer,"* one can add support for a HTTP/2 server in a net/http Server. This can be done as shown below:

func ConfigureServer(s *http.Server,conf *Server) error

The *"conf"* configuration can be set to nil. The above method has to be called before the beginning of execution of the s.

The method *"ConfigureSupport"* is used for configuring a Transport of type net/http HTTP/1 Transport to make use of HTTP/2. It can be used as shown below:

func ConfigureTransport(t1 *http.Transport) error

For the function to work, it requires version 1.6 and above. If it finds an older version, it returns an error.

type clientConn

This can be used as shown below:

```
type ClientConn struct {
  // this has filtered or unexported fields
}
```
The clientConn will just show us the status of a single HTTP/2 client which has been connected to an HTTP/2 server.

type ClientConnPool

This can be used as shown below:

```
type ClientConnPool interface {
  GetClientConn(req    *http.Request,    addr    string)
(*ClientConn,error)
  MarkDead(*ClientConn)
}
```

type ContinuationFrame
This can be used as shown below:

```
type ContinuationFrame struct {
  FrameHeader
  // has the filtered or unexported fields
}
```

This type is used for the purpose of continuing a sequence of fragments of header blocks.
type DataFrame
This can be used as shown below:

```
type DataFrame struct {
  FrameData
  // has a filtered or unexported fields
}
```

type ErrCode

This is shown below:

type ErrCode uint32

This gives an error as shown below:

```
const (
  ErrCodeNo              ErrCode = 0x0
  ErrCodeProtocol        ErrCode = 0x1
  ErrCodeInternal        ErrCode = 0x2
  ErrCodeFlowControl     ErrCode = 0x3
  ErrCodeSettingsTimeout ErrCode = 0x4
  ErrCodeStreamClosed    ErrCode = 0x5
  ErrCodeFrameSize       ErrCode = 0x6
  ErrCodeRefusedStream   ErrCode = 0x7
  ErrCodeCancel          ErrCode = 0x8
  ErrCodeCompression     ErrCode = 0x9
  ErrCodeConnect         ErrCode = 0xa
  ErrCodeEnhanceYourCalm ErrCode = 0xb
  ErrCodeInadequateSecurity ErrCode = 0xc
  ErrCodeHTTP11Required  ErrCode = 0xd
)
```

type Flags

This takes the syntax given below:

type Flags uint8

The type of a frame usually determines the meaning of a flag. Consider the example given below:

```
const (
  // A Data Frame
  FlagDataEndStream Flags = 0x1
  FlagDataPadded   Flags = 0x8

  // Headers Frame
  FlagHeadersEndStream  Flags = 0x1
  FlagHeadersEndHeaders Flags = 0x4
  FlagHeadersPadded   Flags = 0x8
  FlagHeadersPriority  Flags = 0x20
  // The Settings Frame
  FlagSettingsAck Flags = 0x1
  // The Ping Frame
  FlagPingAck Flags = 0x1
  // A Continuation Frame
  FlagContinuationEndHeaders Flags= 0x4

  FlagPushPromiseEndHeaders Flags = 0x4
  FlagPushPromisePadded   Flags = 0x8
)
```

type FrameHeader
This can be used as shown below:
```
type FrameHeader struct {
  // Type is a frame type of 1 byte. There exist 10 standard frame
  // types, but the extension frame types can be written by WriteRawFrame
```

// and will then be returned by the ReadFrame (as UnknownFrame).

Type FrameType
// Flags are 1 byte of the 8 potential bit flags per frame.
// They are unique to the frame type.
Flags Flags
// Length represents the length of our frame, excluding the 9 byte header.
// The maximum size should be a one byte less than 16MB (uint24), but //only up to 16KB of frames are allowed without a peer agreement.

Length uint32s
// StreamID is the stream which this frame is for. Some frames
// are not specific to streams, in which case the field is 0.
StreamID uint32
// has filtered or unexported fields
}

type FrameType
This takes the syntax given below:
type FrameType uint8

A FrameType is just a frame which has been registered. This is shown in the code given below:

```
const (
  FrameData       FrameType = 0x0
  FrameHeaders    FrameType = 0x1
  FramePriority   FrameType = 0x2
  FrameRSTStream  FrameType = 0x3
  FrameSettings   FrameType = 0x4
  FramePushPromise FrameType = 0x5
  FramePing       FrameType = 0x6
  FrameGoAway     FrameType = 0x7
  FrameWindowUpdate FrameType = 0x8
  FrameContinuation FrameType = 0x9
)
```

This is just used to represent an HTTP/2 setting. Consider the example given below:

```
const (
  SettingHeaderTableSize    SettingID = 0x1
  SettingEnablePush         SettingID = 0x2
  SettingMaxConcurrentStreams SettingID = 0x3
  SettingInitialWindowSize  SettingID = 0x4
  SettingMaxFrameSize       SettingID = 0x5
  SettingMaxHeaderListSize  SettingID = 0x6
)
```

Chapter 4- Template Blocks

In Go 1.6, there are two new features introduced in the use of templates. This version of the Go programming language has made it easier for us to trim the spaces around our template actions, and this feature will make the definitions of our templates be more readable.

When a minus sign is placed at the beginning of an action, this is an indication that the space found before the action should first be trimmed. If the minus is placed at the end of the action, this is an indication that the space after the action should be trimmed.

Consider the template given below:

{{20 -}}
<
{{- 50}}

The above template should format to 20<50.

Also, it has become possible for us to replace some pieces of templates by use of the {{block}}action. However, this has to be combined with other redefinitions of templates.

The template package in Go 1.6 has a new feature named block. This block has been designed so that it can work in the same manner as a template, but this provides us with a default value which we can use the "*define*" actions so as to overwrite. However, in the case of templates, we are not provided with a default value, and we have to provide the default action.

We need to demonstrate these using two pages, that is, the Home and the About pages. We will also make use of two templates in our example. The template with the name "*base*" will define the structure of our page. The template named "*content*" will have the content for our page.

Content Templates

Each content templates that we have will correspond to a page. Here is the template for the home page, that is, home.tmpl:

```
{{define "title"}}Home{{end}}
{{define "content"}}This is our Home page.{{end}}
```

Here is the template for the About page, that is, about.tmpl:

```
{{define "title"}}About{{end}}
{{define "content"}}This is our About page.{{end}}
```

The base template, that is, base.tmpl, should be as follows:

```
<title>{{template "title" .}}</title>
<body>{{template "content" .}}</body>
```

Code to Render

In the example which is to be given, the base template will be passed in to the function "ParseFiles()" as the first argument, while the content template will be passed in as the second argument. The order here matters, as if you reverse this, nothing will be displayed to the user. The following order can be used for rendering the home page:

```
t, error := template.ParseFiles("base.tmpl", "home.tmpl")
if error != nil {
      log.Fatal(error)
}
if error := t.Execute(os.Stdout, nil); error != nil {
      log.Fatal(error)
}
```

With the above, the about page will render as shown below:

```
<title>About</title>
<body>This is our about page.</body>
```

You have to note that there are limits to a template action. Consider a website in which you have 500 content templates. For you to add a footer section to the template *"base.tmpl"* which will pull the content from the content templates, one should go through the content templates, the 500 of them, and then add a define action to the templates, otherwise, you will get the error given below:

```
no such template "footer"
```

New Block

It is now time for us to convert the template actions to get block actions. There is no need for us to make any changes to the content templates. Just update the base template so that it appears as shown below:

```
<title>{{block "title" .}}The Default
Title{{end}}</title>
<body>{{block "content" .}}This is our default
body.{{end}}</body>
```

In the case of a matching define for the content template, then the default content will be displayed.

Chapter 5- Language Matching

The Go language enables us to make a decision on the language which is to be used for publishing data in the Unicode CLDR (Common Locale Data Repository).

Consider the example given below, which shows how the language preferences of a user can be matched with the supported languages of the application. Here is the code for the example:

```go
package main
import (
  "fmt"
  "golang.org/x/text/language"
  "golang.org/x/text/language/display"
)
var uPrefs = []language.Tag{
  language.Make("gsw"), // Swiss German
  language.Make("fr"),  // French
}
var servLangs = []language.Tag{
  language.AmericanEnglish, // en-US fallback
  language.German,        // de
}
var matcher = language.NewMatcher(servLangs)
func main() {
  tag, index, confidence := matcher.Match(uPrefs...)

  fmt.Printf("best    match:    %s    (%s)    index=%d
confidence=%v\n",
     display.English.Tags().Name(tag),
     display.Self.Name(tag),
     index, confidence)
  // best    match:    German    (Deutsch)    index=1
confidence=High
}
```

Creation of Language Tags

This can simply be done by use of the language, and this will help us create a tag from the user-driven language tag string.

Make will not return an error. In most cases, the default setting is that if an error is returned, then the default language should be returned. This has made it more convenient for users. Parse can be used for the purpose of handling errors manually.

The header "Accept-Language" used in HTTP is for the purpose of passing the desired languages of a user. This makes it more convenient for the users. If you need to handle errors manually, then make use of Parse. The default setting is that the language pack will not canonicalize tags. When tags are canonicalized in Go, some useful information about our intent is lost. The process of canonicalization is handled in the Matcher. The user is also provided with a full array of canonicalization options if they desire to have it.

How to Match User-preferred Languages to the supported Languages

For us to match the user preferred languages to the supported languages, we use a matcher. If you don't need to deal with all the problems associated with matching languages, it is strongly recommended that you use the matcha.

The method for matching may pass through the user settings from our preferred tags to the supported tag which has been selected. The tag which we get from the match is usually used for getting the resources which are specific to the language.

To initialize a matcha, we use the languages which are supported by the application, and in most cases, these are the languages which have translations. The set in this case has been fixed, and this gives us room to create a matcha at startup. The Matcher has been optimized so that it can improve the performance of the matcha, but this is paid for in terms of increased initialization cost.

The language package provides us with a predefined set of language tags which are mostly used and we can use these for the purpose of defining the supported set. The users are not required to worry about the tags which they should pick for the supported languages.

Consider the matcha given below which can be used for displaying the list of languages which are supported:

```
var supported = []language.Tag{
  language.AmericanEnglish,     // en-US: first
language is fallback
   language.German,        // de
   language.Dutch,       // nl
   language.Portuguese        // pt (defaults to
Brazilian)
   language.EuropeanPortuguese, // pt-pT
   language.Romanian        // ro
```

```go
    language.Serbian,          // sr (defaults to Cyrillic
script)
    language.SerbianLatin,      // sr-Latn
    language.SimplifiedChinese, // zh-Hans
    language.TraditionalChinese, // zh-Hant
}
var matcher = language.NewMatcher(supported)
```

Consider the next example given below, which shows how supported languages can be displayed:

```go
var supported = []language.Tag{
    language.English,          // en
    language.French,           // fr
    language.Dutch,            // nl
    language.Make("nl-BE"),     // nl-BE
    language.SimplifiedChinese, // zh-Hans
    language.TraditionalChinese, // zh-Hant
    language.Russian,          // ru
  }
  en := display.English.Tags()
  for _, t := range supported {
    fmt.Printf("%-20s        (%s)\n",         en.Name(t),
display.Self.Name(t))
  }
```

When you execute the above code, you will get the following as the output:

```
English        (English)
French         (français)
Dutch          (Nederlands)
Flemish        (Vlaams)
Simplified Chinese  (简体中文)
Traditional Chinese  (繁體中文)
Russian        (русский)
```

Chapter 6- Sorting

In Go version 1.6, the sort has been implemented in such a way that we make 10% fewer calls to our Less and Swap methods of the interface, which correspond to the overall time savings. With the new algorithm, a different method for ordering is chosen than we did before for the values which are comparing equal and less.

With this, we are not guaranteed of the final order of the values which are equal, but for the case of programs expecting a specific order, this may not be good.

With the sort package, we are provided with primitives which we can use to sort slices and collections which have been defined by users. Consider the example given below:

```go
package main
import (
        "fmt"
        "sort"
)
type Student struct {
        Name string
        Age  int
}
func (s Student) String() string {
        return fmt.Sprintf("%s: %d", s.Name, s.Age)
}
// ByAge will implement sort.Interface for []Student based on
// the field for Age.
type ByAge []Student
func (x ByAge) Len() int        { return len(x) }
func (x ByAge) Swap(i, j int)    { x[i], x[j] = x[j], x[i] }
func (x ByAge) Less(i, j int) bool { return x[i].Age < x[j].Age }
func main() {
        people := []Student{
```

```go
        {"Joel", 28},
        {"John", 40},
        {"Michael", 17},
        {"Mercy", 22},
    }
    fmt.Println(people)
    sort.Sort(ByAge(people))
    fmt.Println(people)
}
```

A programmable sort criteria can also be used for sorting a struct type. Consider the example given below which shows how this can be done:

```go
package main

import (
        "fmt"
        "sort"
)
// A couple of the type definitions for making the units clear.
type earthMass float64
type au float64
// A Planet is for defining the properties of the solar system object.
type Planet struct {
        name    string
        mass    earthMass
        distance ax
}
// The By will be the type of a "less" function which defines how ordering of the Planet arguments will be done.
type By func(p1, p2 *Planet) bool
// Sort is the method on our function type, By, which will sort the argument slice based on the function.
func (by By) Sort(planets []Planet) {
        ps := &planetSorter{
                planets: planets,
```

```go
            by:      by, // The receiver for the Sort
method is the function (closure) which defines the
sort order.
    }
    sort.Sort(ps)
}
// planetSorter will join a By function and the slice of
Planets which is to be sorted.
type planetSorter struct {
    planets []Planet
    by      func(p1, p2 *Planet) bool // The Closure
used for the Less method.
}
// Len is a part of the sort.Interface.
func (s *planetSorter) Len() int {
    return len(s.planets)
}
// The Swap will be part of the sort.Interface.
func (s *planetSorter) Swap(i, j int) {
    s.planets[i],    s.planets[j]    =    s.planets[j],
s.planets[i]
}
// The Less is part of the sort.Interface. We
implemented this by calling closure "by" in the sorter.
func (s *planetSorter) Less(i, j int) bool {
    return s.by(&s.planets[i], &s.planets[j])
}
var planets = []Planet{
    {"Mercury", 0.055, 0.4},
    {"Venus", 0.815, 0.7},
    {"Earth", 1.0, 1.0},
    {"Mars", 0.107, 1.5},
}
func main() {
    // The Closures which order the Planet
structure.
    name := func(p1, p2 *Planet) bool {
        return p1.name < p2.name
    }
```

```go
    mass := func(p1, p2 *Planet) bool {
        return p1.mass < p2.mass
    }
    distance := func(p1, p2 *Planet) bool {
        return p1.distance < p2.distance
    }
    decreasingDistance := func(p1, p2 *Planet) bool
{

        return !distance(p1, p2)
    }

    // Sorting the planets based on the various
criteria.
    By(name).Sort(planets)
    fmt.Println("By name:", planets)
    By(mass).Sort(planets)
    fmt.Println("By mass:", planets)
    By(distance).Sort(planets)
    fmt.Println("By distance:", planets)
    By(decreasingDistance).Sort(planets)
    fmt.Println("By decreasing distance:", planets)
}
```

Different sets of multiple fields can be used for sorting a struct type. The code given below demonstrates how this can be done:

```go
package main
import (
    "fmt"
    "sort"
)

type Change struct {
    user    string
    language string
    lines   int
}
type lessFunc func(f1, f2 *Change) bool
```

```go
type multiSorter struct {
	changes []Change
	less    []lessFunc
}
func (ms *multiSorter) Sort(changes []Change) {
	ms.changes = changes
	sort.Sort(ms)
}
func OrderedBy(less ...lessFunc) *multiSorter {
	return &multiSorter{
		less: less,
	}
}
func (ms *multiSorter) Len() int {
	return len(ms.changes)
}
func (ms *multiSorter) Swap(i, j int) {
	ms.changes[i], ms.changes[j] = ms.changes[j], ms.changes[i]
}
func (ms *multiSorter) Less(i, j int) bool {
	p, q := &ms.changes[i], &ms.changes[j]
		var k int
	for k = 0; k < len(ms.less)-1; k++ {
		less := ms.less[k]
		switch {
		case less(p, q):
					return true
		case less(q, p):

				return false
		}
			}
		return ms.less[k](p, q)
}
var changes = []Change{
	{"gri", "Go", 120},
	{"ken", "C", 130},
	{"glenda", "Go", 150},
```

```go
        {"rsc", "Go", 250},
        {"r", "Go", 100},
        {"ken", "Go", 210},
        {"dmr", "C", 110},
        {"r", "C", 140},
        {"gri", "Smalltalk", 80},
}
func main() {
        user := func(j1, j2 *Change) bool {
                return j1.user < j2.user
        }
        language := func(j1, j2 *Change) bool {
                return j1.language < j2.language
        }
        increasingLines := func(j1, j2 *Change) bool {
                return j1.lines < j2.lines
        }
        decreasingLines := func(j1, j2 *Change) bool {
                return j1.lines > j2.lines // Note: > orders downwards.
        }
                OrderedBy(user).Sort(changes)
        fmt.Println("By user:", changes)
        OrderedBy(user,
increasingLines).Sort(changes)
        fmt.Println("By user,<lines:", changes)
        OrderedBy(user,
decreasingLines).Sort(changes)
        fmt.Println("By user,>lines:", changes)

        OrderedBy(language,
increasingLines).Sort(changes)
        fmt.Println("By language,<lines:", changes)
        OrderedBy(language,          increasingLines,
user).Sort(changes)
        fmt.Println("By          language,<lines,user:",
changes)
}
```

The example given below shows how a SortWrapper can be used:

```go
package main
import (
        "fmt"
        "sort"
)
type Grams int
func (gr Grams) String() string { return fmt.Sprintf("%dg", int(gr)) }
type Organ struct {
        Name   string
        Weight Grams
}
type Organs []*Organ
func (orgs Organs) Len() int     { return len(orgs) }
func (orgs Organs) Swap(i, j int) { s[i], s[j] = s[j], s[i] }
// ByName will implement the sort.Interface by
providing the Less and using Len and Swap methods
of our embedded Organs value.
type ByName struct{ Organs }
func (orgs ByName) Less(i, j int) bool { return
orgs.Organs[i].Name < orgs.Organs[j].Name }
// ByWeight will implement the sort.Interface by
providing the Less and //use the Len and the Swap
methods of the embedded Organs value.
type ByWeight struct{ Organs }
func (orgs ByWeight) Less(i, j int) bool { return
orgs.Organs[i].Weight < orgs.Organs[j].Weight }
func main() {
        orgs := []*Organ{
                {"spleen", 150},
                {"brain", 1350},
                {"liver", 1480},
                {"pancreas", 142},
                {"heart", 270},
                {"prostate", 59},
                }
```

```go
        sort.Sort(ByWeight{orgs})
        fmt.Println("Organs by weight:")
        printOrgans(orgs)
        sort.Sort(ByName{orgs})
        fmt.Println("Organs by name:")
        printOrgans(orgs)
}
func printOrgans(s []*Organ) {
        for _, o := range orgs {
                fmt.Printf("%-8s      (%v)\n",      o.Name,
o.Weight)
        }
}
```

Let us discuss some of the functions associated with this.

func Search

This takes the syntax given below:

func Search(n int, f func(int) bool)int

It makes use of a binary search so as to return the smallest index. Consider the example given below:

```go
y := 20
i := sort.Search(len(data), func(i int) bool { return
data[i] >= y })
if i < len(data) && data[i] == y {
        // y is present at position data[i]
} else {
        // y is not available in data,
        // but i is our index where it should be inserted.
}
```
In the above case, the data has been sorted in an ascending order, and we are in need of finding the value y in the integer. Consider the example given below which shows how one can guess for a number:

```
func GuessGame() {
    var x string
    fmt.Printf("Select an integer between 0 and
100.\n")
    answer := sort.Search(100, func(i int) bool {
        fmt.Printf("Is your number <= %d? ", i)
        fmt.Scanf("%x", &x)
        return x != "" && x[0] == 'y'
    })
    fmt.Printf("The number is %d.\n", answer)
}
```

type Interface

This can be used as shown below:

```
type Interface interface {
    // The Len is a number representing elements in
the collection.
    Len() int
    // Less will report on whether the element having
    // index i is expected to sort before the element
having index j.
    Less(i, j int) bool
    // Swap will swap the elements having indexes i
and j.
    Swap(i, j int)
}
```

A type which is able to satisfy the sort.Interface can be sorted by use of the routines which are contained in the package. For this to work, the elements have to be enumerated by use of an index of type integer.

Chapter 7- Package Reflect

There was incompatibility between gcc and gccgo in the previous version of the Go programming language. However, Go 1.6 has come in to resolve this problem. For this package to be used within a program, we have to import it as shown below:

import "reflect"

With this package, a program can be in a position to manipulate objects which have arbitrary types. Let us discuss some of the functions found in this package, and how they are used.

func Copy

This is implemented using the following syntax:

func Copy(dst, src Value) int

This function is used for copying the contents of a src folder to the dst folder. Once the copying has been done, the number of elements which have been copied will be returned.

func Select

This takes the following syntax when it is to be used:

func Select(cases []SelectCase) (chosen int, recv Value, recvOK bool)

This function will execute a select operation which has been described in the list of the cases. Just like the select statement in Go, the blocking will be done until one of the cases is in a position to proceed, and then a pseudo-random choice is the made. Lastly, the case is then executed.

type ChanDir

This takes the syntax given below:

type ChanDir int

CharDir is used to represent the type direction of a channel. This is shown in the code given below:

```
const (
    RecvDir ChanDir      = 1 << iota // <-chan
    SendDir               // chan<-
    BothDir = RecvDir | $endDir      // chan
)
```

type Kind

This is used with the syntax given below:

type Kind uint

A kind is used for representing the particular kind of type that is used for representing a Type. Zero kind is not considered to be a valid kind. Consider the code given below:

```
const (
    Invalid kind = iota
    Bool
    Int
    Int8
    Int16
    Int32
    Int64
    Uint
    Uint8
    Uint16
    Uint32
    Uint64
    Uintptr
    Float32
    Float64
    Complex64
    Complex128
    Array
    Chan
    Func
    Interface
    Map
    Ptr
    Slice
    String
    Struct
    UnsafePointer
)
```

type Method

The code given below shows how this type can be used:

```
type Method struct {
    // Name is the name of our method.
    // PkgPath is the path to our package that qualifies
a lower case (unexported)

    // method name.  This is empty for the upper case
method names.

    // When we combine the PkgPath and the Name is
uniquely identifying //a method in a method set.

    Name   string
    PkgPath string
    Type  Type  // the method type
    Func Value // func with a receiver as the first
argument
    Index int  // index for the Type.Method
}
```

The method will represent a single method.

type SelectCase
This is used as shown below:
type SelectCase struct {
    Dir SelectDir // direction of the case
    Chan Value   // The channel to use for the purpose of send or receive

    Send Value   // The value to send (for the send)
}
This is used for the purpose of describing a single case in a particular select operation. The Dir usually determines the kind of case which is to be used, and this is the direction of the communication process. If the Dir is set to SelectDefault, the case will be representing a default case. The value for Chan and Send should be set to zero.

If the Dir is set to SelectSend, the case will be representing a send operation. The underlying value for Chan must be a channel, and the underlying value for Send should be assignable to the element type of the channel. If the value of Chan is zero, the case is normally ignored, and the Send field will also be ignored and its value can be either a zero or a non-zero.

type SelectDir
This is used with the syntax given below:
type SelectDir int

A SelectDir is used for describing the direction of the communication of a select case. This is shown in the code given below:
const (
    _   SelectDir = iota
    SelectSend   // case Chan <- Send
    SelectRecv   // case <-Chan:
    SelectDefault   // default
)

type SliceHeader

This can be used as shown in the code below:

```
type SliceHeader struct {
    Data uintptr
    Len  int
    Cap int
}
```

This is used for the purpose of representing slice during runtime. This one cannot be used portably or safely and the representation of this may change with future releases. Also, the field for the data is not enough to guarantee us that the data which is being referenced will not be garbage collected, and therefore the programs have to keep a typed pointer which is separate and typed correctly to the underlying data.

type StringHeader

This one can be used as shown below:

```
type StringHeader struct {
    Data uintptr
    Len int
}
```

The StringHeader is used for representing a string during runtime. It is hard for us to represent this one portably or correctly as it may change later on. Also, the data field does not guarantee us that the data which it is representing will not be garbage collected, and this is why programs have to keep a pointer which is correctly and strongly typed to the data which is underlying.

type StructField

This can be used as shown below:

```
type StructField struct {
    // Name is name of the field.
    Name string
    // PkgPath is our package path which qualifies a lower case
    // field name. This is empty for an upper case field names (exported).
    PkgPath string
    Type    Type      // the type of field
    Tag     StructTag // the field tag string
    Offset  uintptr   // the offset within the struct, in bytes
    Index   []int     // the index sequence for the Type.FieldByIndex
    Anonymous bool    // this is an embedded field
}
```

A StructField is used for describing a single field which is contained in a struct.

type Type

This can be used as shown below:

```
type Type interface {
    // Align will return the alignment in bytes of the value of
    // the type once allocated in memory.
    Align() int
    // FieldAlign will return alignment in bytes of the value of
    // the type once used as the field in a struct.
    FieldAlign() int
    // Method will return the i'th method in our type's method set.
    // It will panic in case the i is not in the range [0, NumMethod()).
    Func
```

Method(int) Method
// MethodByName will return the method with the name in the type's
// method set and boolean which indicates whether the method was found.
MethodByName(string) (Method, bool)
// NumMethod will return the number of the methods in the type's method set.

NumMethod() int
// Name will return the type's name within the package.
// It will return an empty string for our unnamed types.
Name() string
// PkgPath will return named type's package path, which is the import //path which uniquely identifies our package, such as the //"encoding/base64".

// If the type had been predeclared (string, error) or maybe unnamed (*T, struct{}, []int),

// our package path will just be an empty string.
PkgPath() string
// The Size will return the number of bytes which are needed for storing
// a value of given type; and it's analogous to unsafe.Sizeof.
Size() uintptr
// The String will return a string representation of type.
// The string representation can be used in shortened package names
// and it is not a guaranteed for it to be unique among the types. For us //to test for equality, just compare the Types directly.

String() string

// The Kind will return the specific kind of our type.
Kind() Kind
// Implements will report whether the type is implementing the //interface type u.
Implements(u Type) bool
// AssignableTo will report if a value of the type is assignable to the type //u.
AssignableTo(u Type) bool
// ConvertibleTo will report if a value of the type is convertible to the //type u.
ConvertibleTo(u Type) bool
// Comparable will report if the values of the type are comparable.
Comparable() bool
// Bits will return the size of our type in bits.
// It will panic in case the type's Kind is not within the
// sized or unsized Uint, Int, Float, or Complex types.
Bits() int
// ChanDir will return the direction of a channel type.
// It will panic if the Kind of type is not Chan.
ChanDir() ChanDir
// IsVariadic will report whether a type of a function final input //parameter is a parameter of "..." If so, t.In(t.NumIn() - 1) will return the

// implicit actual type []T of parameter
// To be concrete, if t represents a func(x int, y ... float64), then
//   t.NumIn() == 2
// t.In(0) will be the reflect.Type for "int"
// t.In(1) will be the reflect.Type for "[]float64"
// t.IsVariadic() == true
// IsVariadic will panic if the Kind of type is not Func.
IsVariadic() bool

// Elem will return an element type of Kind.
// It will panic if the Kind of type is not Chan, Array, Map, Ptr, or Slice.

Elem() Type
// Field will return a struct i'th field of type.
// It will panic if the Kind of type is not Struct.
// It will panic if the i is not in range of [0, NumField()).
Field(I int) StructField
// FieldByIndex will return the nested field which corresponds
// to the index sequence. It's equivalent to the calling Field
// successively for each of the index i.
// It will panic if the Kind of type is not Struct.
FieldByIndex(index []int) StructField
// FieldByName will return the struct field having the given name
// and a boolean which indicates whether the field was found.
FieldByName(name string) (StructField, bool)
// FieldByNameFunc will return the first struct field having a name
// which satisfies the match function and the boolean which indicates //whether the field was found.

FieldByNameFunc(match func(string) bool) (StructField, bool)
// In will return the type of the function i'th type input parameter.
// It will panic if the Kind of type is not Func.
// It will panic if i is not in range of [0, NumIn()).
In(I int) Type
// The Key will return a map key type of type.
// It will panic if the Kind of type is not a Map.
Key() Type
// Len will return an array length of type.

```go
    // It will panic if the Kind of type is not Array.
    Len() int
    // NumField will return a struct field count of
type.
    // It will panic if the Kind of type is not Struct.
    NumField() int
    // NumIn will return a function input parameter
count of type.
    // It will panic if the Kind of type is not Func.
    NumIn() int
    // NumOut will return a function output
parameter count of type.
    // It will panic if the Kind of type is not Func.
    NumOut() int
    // Out will return the type of a function i'th output
parameter of type.
    // It will panic if the Kind of type is not Func.
    // It will panic if i is not in range of [0, NumOut()).
    Out(I int) Type
    // has the filtered or unexported methods
}
```

type ValueError

This is used as shown below:

type ValueError struct {
    Method string
    Kind kind
}

This usually occurs once a value method has been invoked on a value which does not support it. Each method has a description of such cases.

Chapter 8- Tools

Cgo

This tool experienced one major change, with the other change being minor. The process of defining rules for sharing the Go pointers in a C code has been changed, and this has made it possible for the C code to exist together with the garbage collector in Go. You have to note that it is possible for Go and C to share the same memory which has been allocated by Go once a pointer to that memory has been passed to the C as part of the cgo call, and the memory itself should not have pointers to the memory which Go-allocated, and that the C will not retain the pointer once the call has returned a value.

The runtime is responsible for checking for the rules during the execution of the program. If a violation is detected by the runtime, then a diagnosis is displayed and the program crashes. If you are in need of disabling these checks, you just have to set the environment variable *"GODEBUG=cgocheck=0."* However, before making this change, it is good for you to take note that the majority of the code is incompatible with garbage collection maybe in one way or another. If you disable the checks, you will cause more failures which are mysterious. It will be good for you to choose fixing of the code in question rather than having to disable the checks which can lead to more serious issues.

The minor change brought to Cgo was the introduction of the explicit *"C.complexdouble"* and *"C.complexfloat"* types, and these are separate from complex128 and complex64 in Go. Currently, matching of the other numeric types which include Go's complex type and C's complex types are not interchangeable.

Go doc command

The Go doc command was introduced in Go 1.5, and it allows us to make references to packages using only the name of the package, as it is done in go doc http. In case ambiguity occurs, the Go 1.5 will make use of the package with a lexicographically import path. If ambiguity occurs in Go 1.6, it is resolved by preferring the import paths having fewer elements, and the ties are broken using a lexicographic comparison. A very important effect of the change is that the original copies of the packages will be preferred to the vendored copies. The successful copies will also run a bit faster.

To import the doc package in Go, we use the following command:

import "go/doc"

In this package, variables are declared as shown below:

```
var IllegalPrefixes = []string{
    "copyright",
    "all rights",
    "author",
}
```

type Example

This can be used as shown below:

```
type Example struct {
    Name        string // the name of item being exemplified
    Doc     string // an example of function doc string
    Code    ast.Node
    Play        *ast.File // the whole program version of an example
    Comments    []*ast.CommentGroup
    Output      string // the expected output
    EmptyOutput bool   // we expect empty output
    Order       int    // the order of the original source code order
}
```

type Func

This can be used as shown below:

type Func struct {
    Doc string
    Name string
    Decl 8ast.Func.Decl
        Recv string // the actual receiver "T" or "*T"
    Orig string // the original receiver of "T" or "*T"
    Level int // the embedding level; 0 will mean not embedded
}

type Mode

This is used with the following syntax:

type Mode int

The mode values are used for the purpose of controlling how New flows. This is shown below:

const (
    // the extract documentation for all the package-level declarations,
    // but not just the exported ones
    AllDecls Mode = 1 << iota
    // showing all the embedded methods, not just ones of
    //the invisible anonymous fields (unexported)
    AllMethods
)

Type Node

This can be used as follows:

type Note struct {
    Pos, End token.pos // the position range of a comment having the marker
    UID   string // uid found with our marker
    Body string // note the body text

}
In Go, a Note is used for representing a comment which has been marked.

type Package
This can be used as shown below:

```
type Package struct {
    Doc      string
    Name     string
    ImportPath string
    Imports  []string
    Filenames []string
    Notes    map[string][]*Note
    // Deprecated: For the sake of backward
compatibility Bugs is still being //populated,
    // but all the new code should make use of Notes
instead.
    Bugs []string
    // declarations
    Consts []*Value
    Types []*Type
    Vars []*Value
    Funcs []*Func
}
```
The package provides the documentation for the entire package.

type Type

This can be used as shown below:

```
type Type struct {
    Doc string
    Name string
    Decl *ast.GenDecl

    // the associated declarations
```

Consts []*Value // the sorted list of the constants of this type
Vars   []*Value // the sorted list of the variables of (mostly) this type
Funcs   []*Func // the sorted list of the functions returning the type
Methods []*Func // the sorted list of the methods (including the //embedded ones) of the type
}

Type is just a declaration of the type declaration.
type Value
This can be used as shown below:

type Value struct {
Doc string
Names []string // the var or the const names in a declaration order
Decl *ast.GenDecl
// has the filtered or unexported fields
}

The value is used for representation of the documentation for a const or variable declaration.

Compiler Toolchain

This tool has been left almost unchanged. The internal change to it is that the parser has not been hand-written rather than being generated by yacc as it was done previously.

A new flag, "-*msan*" has been introduced to the linker, compiler, and go command, which is analogous to the "–*race*," and this is only available to Linux/amd64, and this is good for enabling interoperability with MemorySanitizer. This kind of interoperation is very good when it comes to testing a program with C or C++ code.

The linker now has a new option named "-libgcc" and this is used for setting the location where we expect to have our C compiler support library whenever we are linking the cgo code. This option will be consulted only when we are using linkmode=internal, and if we are in need of disabling the support for a library, we can set it to "*none.*"

Ports

In Go 1.6, experimental ports have been added to Linux 64-bit MIPS. These ports are in support of cgo but with internal linking. Go 1.6 has also added an experimental port to Android on a 32-bit x86. In the case of FreeBSD, Go 1.6 has turned into using clang rather than the gcc, and this is used as the external compiler. On Linux/ppc64le, cgo is now supported in Go 1.6 together with external linking, and the feature is roughly complete. On Nacl, Go 1.6 has brought about support for later versions of SDKs.

Performance

The changes in terms of performance in Go 1.6 are so general and do vary, such that it is difficult for us to make precise statements about the performance of the language. It has been found that the programs found in Go benchmark suite 1 run a bit faster in Go 1.6 than in Go 1.5. In Go 1.5, we had more pauses for the garbage collector. These pauses have been reduced in Go 1.6. This is the case mostly in programs which make use of large sizes of memory.

Changes to the Library

In Go 1.6, only minor changes were brought to the library. Some of these minor changes include the following:

1. The packages **compress/gzip**, **compress/flate**, and **compress/zlib** can now report **io.ErrUnexpectedEOF** for input streams which are truncated, rather than **io.EOF**.

2. The package **crypto/cipher** can now overwrite the destination buffer in case the decryption of the GCM fails. This is for the purpose of allowing the AESNI code avoid using any temporary buffer.

3. The package **encoding/asn1** can now export the class and tag constants which are normally used when we need to parse ASN.1 structures which are advanced.

4. In the package math/big, Int will add the Append and the Text methods which will add more control to the user whenever they are printing.

Conclusion

It can be concluded that the Go programming language is a very good language. Recently, version 1.6 of Go was introduced. This introduced a number of changes in how things are done and support for new features in Go. The library experienced a number of changes after the introduction of this version of the Go programming language. However, the specification of the language did not change in any way. This means that in terms of specification, things are done in the same way they were done in the previous versions of the Go.

There are new ports which have been introduced in Go 1.6, and these are mostly for operating systems for Android and Linux. Experimental ports, which are very important to operating systems such as Linux were introduced in Go 1.6, meaning that the user can perform a number of tasks with these. The tool "*Cgo*" also received a change in Go 1.6. The rules which define how Go pointers are shared with C code have been changed, meaning that a change in how this is done will be experienced.

The Compiler ToolChain was left st almounchanged. However, the main change in this was done internally in that the parser is now being handwritten rather than being generated by the yacc (yet another compiler). A new flag has also been introduced to the go command, compiler, and the link, and these have a great effect on how things are being done in Go programming language.

The protocol HTTP/2 is now supported in Go, both in servers and in clients. The support for this has been transparently added. Concurrent apps are normally misused in Go. In Go 1.6, this will easily be detected during runtime, and the necessary action will be taken.